LIFE VIEW

by Jenny Durr

RED LEAD PRESS
PITTSBURGH, PENNSYLVANIA 15222

The contents of this work including, but not limited to, the accuracy of events, people, and places depicted; opinions expressed; permission to use previously published materials included; and any advice given or actions advocated are solely the responsibility of the author, who assumes all liability for said work and indemnifies the publisher against any claims stemming from publication of the work.

ISBN: 978-1-4349-6461-8
eISBN: 978-1-4349-4697-3
Printed in the United States of America

First Printing

For more information or to order additional books, please contact:
Red Lead Press
701 Smithfield Street
Pittsburgh, Pennsylvania 15222
U.S.A.
1-800-834-1803
www.redleadbooks.com

ABOUT THE AUTHOR

AT THE TIME OF PUBLICATION, JENNY DURR IS FORTY years old. She started writing at the age of seven. She dictates her work because she has Cerebral Palsy and is in a wheelchair. She currently lives in central New Jersey, near her childhood home.

The author spent her childhood living in the country with her parents and sister. Her father recently retired from farming after forty years.

The author's entire schooling was at a special ed. school. Her favorite subject was and continues to be English. Her grandmother lovingly took down Jenny's very first poem, "Why, Why, Why?" People have often told the author that she is wise beyond her years as the content of her poetry shows.

ABOUT THE BOOK

THIS BOOK HAS SOMETHING FOR EVERYONE. THE author shows that even with a disability people are multi-faceted and desire to contribute, not only to their world, but to the world as a whole. The author wishes to challenge any pre-conceived notions about disability and offers a new perspective. This book presents powerful writing that will enlighten and stay with the reader.

The author's passion is to share how Jesus Christ has not only helped her cope but gives her life more meaning. The book's range of emotion reminds us that we are all human and need each other. The author's greatest desire is to show, through humor, love, and God's grace, that we can all give something to each other.

ACKNOWLEDGMENTS

FIRST, I WOULD LIKE TO THANK JESUS CHRIST. ANY talent I have has been given to me by Him.

Mom and Dad: I know you said it wasn't necessary to acknowledge you but I wanted to. I love you. Thanks for making me who I am. I appreciate all the time, energy and care you always give me.

Lainie Casper: Thank you for your patience Lainie. Sorry for making you kill your eyes. Thank you for teaching me the importance of how things look on the page to the reader. Thanks for our talks about faith and your wisdom about relationships.

Rose Liedtka: Thank you. It's been a fun 19 years. Even though we didn't work on this project too much together, it's an important step in my writing career and I want to acknowledge you. Thank you for the laughter. Thanks for all the typing and retyping you've done. I know every time I put revised on a poem you probably felt like screaming.

Special thanks to Ellen F., Arts Access first creative writing/journalism instructor. Thank you Ellen for helping me get published for the first time outside of a school newsletter or church bulletin. Thanks to Lyn Sanders, Arts Access Director. Lyn, thanks for making Arts Access what it is today. Thanks to all Arts Access staff especially the facilitators. Although, you did not help me with this book, I wanted to acknowledge you for helping me to express myself in other fields.

Keith Garletts: Thank you for reading over the contract. This is a big step for me. I consider this my first real publishing opportunity except for one magazine article. For that there was no contract.

A special thanks to Eileen Murray. I have done some of my work with other Arts Access staff but the majority of it has been done with whomever I could find to help me at the time. No one has worked with me as long as you have. Thanks for allowing me to dictate more than one piece that is contained in this book. Thanks for those times I was on fire and you burnt your fingers off trying to keep up with me.

Thanks to all the people whom I have dictated to over the years. All of you had a role in this next step in my writing career. Without your willingness to take down what I want to say I would not have any poetry to publish. Thanks to all of you. There are too many to thank here individually.

Silent Voices

Silent people, people with voices,
Painfully loud but oh
How painfully silent.
Waiting for somebody to ask the right question.
Hoping, praying that someone will ask a question
That they can raise their eyes to.

People ask, "Do you hurt?" His eyes go up.
Hoping the listener names the right body part
And hears this silent plea for relief.
He can't say something hurts, but his face says it all.

A well-meaning person forces him to eat.
His eyes are saying, No, No, No.
I hear what's happening, the aide is saying.
"Yes, you have to eat."
Even though I can't see his eyes, I know he is saying no.
Later on as I sit in the hall, I ask, "Did she make you
mad?"

His eyes go up…way up!
This only confirms what I felt.

Then again, even someone who knows him well
Might not know if they don't ask the right question.
He laughs, cries, jokes,
Feels what we feel.
Who are not silent.
But if we, who are not silent,
Don't ask a question that makes his eyes go up
He'll never have a voice.
He'll never be heard.
He'll always be silent.
April 25, 1994
Revised July 15, 2009

Ask Them

I'm sitting in my bedroom,
My aide asks me a question,
And then she says, "Let me ask your niece".
Repeating the same question.

Later, I'm in a restaurant with a co-worker
"I want fish", I say.
Co-worker says, "Maybe you'd like the fried chicken instead,
Have something good for a change".
I think to myself,
Strange, I don't tell you what to order.

In the morning I tell my aide what I want to wear.
Aide says, "You wore that outfit just the other day,
Why don't you wear this instead?"
It sure is odd how having limbs that work
Provide power over us who are disabled.
During a visit with non-verbal friend from church

Aide says, "Tell her I said hello",
And I think to myself
She can hear you
Even though she can't answer you
She's right there, dummy.

Laws provide freedom for us on paper
But they don't really change people;
We are still second-class.
If we don't come out of the box
People have made for us, it's okay.
But, if we do come out
People don't know what to think of us
I have tried to come out
But people still ask *them*.
May 28, 2002
Revised July 15, 2009

Sunny Little Bluebird

The dainty little bluebird
In her dainty little nest
Tend to her young
With love and care.
Mother bluebird smoothes her babies' wings,
Sings and puts them gently against her breast to rest.
Babies wake; their mother has supper
Babies eat heartily.
Mother and young fly up to the nest.
Mother wraps blanket of warm feathers around her
young,
Sings lullaby, tucks her head under her breast
For a night's rest.
April 20, 1983
*Originally published in my school newspaper
May 3, 1997

BABY

(I dedicate this poem to women longing
for children they can't have.)

A baby…all yours.
A baby to hold, to hug, a baby…all yours.
A baby to kiss, to hold, to hug.
No fear of it being taken.
A baby…all yours.
A baby to caress,
Rock when it cries,
Comfort when in pain,
A baby…all yours.
A baby to change dirty diapers,
And to heat up formula for.
Mother's pleasure never to be taken away
Because baby is all yours.

A child to teach and bandage skinned knees.
A child…all yours.

A child to give wisdom and share life with.
A child to give the world.
To make a difference.
But a child…always yours.
May 15, 1996

The Train Bound for Heaven

As I enter the New York train station, I notice two separate tracks. One is going to the left and one is going to the right. I notice that the one on the left is much longer and wider. I watch with curiosity as millions of people go down this track.

I wonder why they choose that track when on the other track there is a man with arms outstretched and with a cross in front of Him. This man is saying, "Please, come to me, please come to the cross". Beyond this cross is a beautiful city with gates of pearls and streets of gold.

Sadly, I watch as only a handful of people kneel in front of this man and His cross.

My heart breaks as people on the other track reach the end of it and land in a fiery lake.

As each person tragically approaches the end of this track, the man's voice becomes louder "Please come to me!"

He is calling to you as well. What train are you taking? Please take the Train Bound for Heaven. If you are on the wrong track, seek Jesus and His path for you and ask Him to show you the meaning of the cross. If you truly understand the meaning of the cross, you will be on the right track. He loves you.
June 21, 1994
Revised May, 2009

THE DAYS AT THE EGG FARM

I HAD A VERY HAPPY CHILDHOOD GOING WITH MY Grandmother to the egg farm. When I went to help my grandmother at the egg farm I watched her wash the eggs. Grandmom would tell me all about the eggs. I can remember the different names of eggs like it was yesterday. Some of the names are: large, jumbo, pee-wee, and pullet. I remember one very fond memory in particular; Grandmom handed me a pee-wee egg. It was cool. She told me not to squeeze it too hard or drop it, but I did squeeze it too hard, dropped it and egg went all over the floor.

I have many memories. Another one is when I used to sit outside the egg farm and watch the children of Grandmom's boss catch butterflies. Later I would eat lunch with Grandmom's boss. She was such a wonderful cook. Other times I would sit in the back room and someone would take my arm and push the heavy egg crates down rollers so they could be put in the refrigerator.

The best memories about the egg farm were just having Mom drop me off and letting me sit there. I used to play with my big can of coins I had collected from people who knew I liked to play with them. I would just sit and chat with Grandmom while she worked. Those were happy times at the egg farm. I will never forget the talks Grandmom and I had. I will never forget those egg farm days.
March 31, 2004

Cool

Cool because of laughter,
Cool because of unique humor.
Cool because we overcome anger with talks.
Cool because of shared feelings.
Cool because we respect.
Cool because we know disagreement can't separate.

Cool because we know each other's thoughts.
Cool because we share deep emotions.
Cool just because we have fun together.

Cool because we don't care what other people say.
Cool because we give to one another.
Cool because we love.
Oct. 2, 1997

TEARS ON HER FACE

Loud, sad wails fill my ears,
I watch her full lips quiver.
Her corn rows even lack bounce.
I question, keep questioning.
She keeps shaking her head,
Not having the privilege of speech.

I stare at her blue switches,
She is too upset to use them
To operate her wheelchair.
I wonder, greatly perplexed.
Finally she nods her head
To one of my questions.

All she wants, all she wants
Is to go home for Christmas.
December 19, 1996
Revised May 22, 2009

FAITH

(Dedicated to the Lord Jesus Christ who
is my source of faith)

An interesting mix, faith and doubt;
Some people blindly accept,
And others question.
Some go away when doubts arise;
Others still accept as children.
What should you do when doubts come?
Give in to fear and confusion?
No,
We don't give in to worry or fear;
Accept the fear and challenge your faith.
For me there cannot be faith
Without doubt.
Doubt makes faith stronger.
August 18, 2003

THEY CALLED YOU BOB
HE CALLED HIM GRANDDAD

You chopped wood with great strength.
Ran after sheep, baled hay.
God gave you powerful strength.
Boy was constantly by your side;
Boy was always there to help.
Boy was more like your son than grandson.

Bob, I never knew you;
You won't ever read this.
But, thank you for raising that boy,
Who called you Granddad.
A special man, a friend whom I love.
December 7, 2006

THE TRUE SHINER

Told to wipe tears, but cause them.
Asked to be light, but bring darkness.
Told to imitate Jesus, instead shame Him.
Discourage, not encourage.

Told to celebrate good fortune,
We walk away jealous.
Asked to weep with, instead stare.
Commanded to comfort, but we chastise.

Expose pain, share secrets.
Thought safe and protected,
But betrayed.

Admonished to lift and share burdens,
But, stay closed and separated.

Trusted friendships begun.
Community built, confidences shared.

Suddenly triviality arrives and tears at bonds.
We don't love, instead we hate.

Told to give to one another,
But we take.
Community once built, now gone.
Trusted friends give no good-bye.

Asked to be like Him,
But, we get in the way.
Called to sacrifice, but ignore commands.
Called to love, yet we judge and lack responsibility.
Afraid to point out improvement needed, so say nothing.
Again, no sacrifice, only selfishness
Looking, looking, searching, searching
Instead, find squabbling.
Don't praise…entertain.
Musical-style arguments abound, but no worship.

Seekers begin to go away;
We were told to bring them in.
Quietly someone rises
I hear them whisper "Christ isn't here".
Silently, just watch them go.

Please don't think our light is true.
Our shine is dull.
Please look to the True Shiner.
September 17, 2007
Revised July 7, 2009

MUSIC

Music is something you can
Dance and swing to.
Music is pretty.
Bells ringing have a clear crystal ring
All through the air.

You dance and you swing
When you hear a good musical beat
And you move your feet.
You shake your feet in time with the beat.
You twist your hips, you shake your knees
And you push around, and you swing around
And you dance on your toes.
That's what I call music.
January 5, 1983

A TRUE MAN

(Dedicated to a former Aide,
Thank you for relieving my pain so many nights.)

A true man encourages, always uplifts.
A true man is not afraid to share his fear.
A true man is not afraid to get involved,
Even though he knows he'll have to watch
Someone suffer without being able to stop it.

A true man is not afraid of tears,
Someone else's or his own.
A true man encourages someone to be realistic,
But to reach for all they can be.

A true man is willing to let someone go,
Even though it hurts.
A true man's hands are strong,
But gentle, relieving pain.

A true man never says,
"Be strong, don't feel that way."
A true man always keeps his word.
A true man gives of himself.
March 4, 1996
Revised July 25, 2009

HIDDEN

PEOPLE SEE OUR BODIES; THEY GET BRIEF GLIMPSES into our mind but those quick insignificant moments don't let them see the desires that burn through our whole soul, like a forest fire.

People think they know our dreams, or think they know how it's best for us to achieve them. But they don't.

We try to give them a glimpse of the spark in our soul, but somehow, like a tightrope walker who just misses the rope by half a second, people miss the spark in our hearts. Some of us don't have things in our lives that turn our hearts on fire, or cause us to suffer anguish if we cannot allow the spark to burn freely.

We can't and shouldn't put down the people who don't have something they are so passionate about, that it threatens to make them an empty dried up brittle shell if that desire is forced to be hidden.

Yes, we have other parts of our lives that we must pay attention to, requiring us to sometimes turn down the fire. But, for people who do have the fire, why should we be forced to hide our talents and our God-given abilities? Our abilities aren't great in themselves. But should those abilities be stifled under a veil of questions and concerns about our physical well being? Questions that never end, like: "Who is your aide tonight? But I thought she was off tonight. They told me they'd be right back to take me to the bathroom…"

We try to cope in this sea of confusion; we need to be in this boarding center because of our physical dependency. But, we have a thirst for independence. Should this thirst, and trying to just survive in a sea of confusion, force us to bury our God-given fire? We might not be able to let our fires burn in exactly the way they want to, but to keep it hidden away, because of other peoples' ideas about who we are, is somehow wrong.

July 15, 1995

Please Touch Me

Jerking, jerking pain.

People around me are afraid.
No touch, no touch.
People around me are afraid,
But it won't hurt me.
They are afraid to hurt themselves.
They won't, they won't.

They're afraid to get involved;
They're afraid they don't know how to help me.
I'm not asking for a relationship,
Just a touch.
November 28, 2006
Revised May 22, 2009

Brain Teaser

This brain teaser won't be of the caliber of
"Why did the chicken cross the road?"
Certainly not a "when they go to heaven" joke.
This riddle may strain your gray matter.

Here we go.
Though asparagus is loaded with this
Most people would rather have a tangier
Taste in their mouth
Chocolate, alcohol, anything but this.

This provides summer fun.

It is contained in compound words.
Words that have brought
Scandal to some, such as Nixon,
And ruin to some, such as Napoleon.
Another compound word clue for the 'fifties'

Do you remember the Jack Parr joke
That made him leave "The Tonight Show"?

Sorry for the generation gap.
But it would not be nice to leave
Whole generations out
From brain-teasing pleasure.
For those of you who are now
Tearing your hair out,
Would this help?
What do beetles and buffalo have in common?

Had enough? Give up?

I thought about putting the answer in
A clever, tricky way to make you think,
And still receive the answer.
But, I thought I would spare you
Any more brain trauma.
The next time you go to the faucet
I bet you'll never think of water the same again.
March 25, 2009

TIME GOING

Seconds,
Minutes,
Hours,
Days.
Seconds,
Minutes,
Hours,
Days.

Clocks go around and around.
Seconds,
Minutes,
Hours,
Days.

Slowly slip by with humdrum activity,
Days turn into nights.
Months into years.

We still seek endless pleasure,
Pleasures that serve ourselves.
What are we doing
With our God-given time?
July 8, 2009

MY TONGUE

I did not write "Power of Words" with power.
Words change things in a second…permanently.
Evil words…spoken in one second.

People appreciate seconds, minutes, hours.
They think deeply about universal issues,
Not realizing what everyday words, in seconds, can
cost.

Tongues can be precious or a curse.
Words can uplift, encourage,
Give a lift to one's soul, or permanently damage.
Why do we remember
The negative, hurtful, damaging words?

My God calls and tells me to be holy.
Words can cause awful fires
Damaging one's circumstances or one's very soul.

My Lord has forgiven me,
He'll continue to work in me,
But my tongue is still poison.
Some words can never go away.
April 29, 2008

HINDRANCE

Tooth, you're not very pleasing,
So I'm afraid you'll have to be leaving.

Tooth, you made my home uncomfortable,
So now you won't have a home.

Why do you fight one another?
Why can't you get along with each other?

If you're not content with this home,
On Thursday you'll have to go roam.
December 10, 1998

EVAN

Joy, tears, laughter.
Joy, tears, laughter.

Caring for others.
Never any other way.
Never any other way.

Love your Shepherd!
Love your Shepherd!

How you loved your mother!
Oh, how you loved her.

You are with your Shepherd now.
But you are not forgotten.

Let us remember love,
Laughter and caring.

Let us remember these lessons
You have taught us, Evan
June 19, 2006
Note: name has been changed

Heart Tomb

Dark, empty void,
No color,
Don't know what to search for.

A specially shaped circle is cut out of our heart.
We try placing food, work, drugs,
And any other human substance in this circle,
Nothing fits.

Jesus gave up Himself
To end our dark empty hopeless void.
Jesus fits this circle.
Nothing else makes us complete.
April 6, 2008
Revised June 24, 2009

CHANGE

Change brings fear;
A little word, *change*.
Many different concepts,
Sometimes good…
Buying a new dress in favorite blue.
Sometimes bad…
Nothing in your wardrobe goes with it.

Receiving a promotion
Can be good or bad change.
Bad change…
Not knowing if you can do
What is expected of you.
Good change…
More money, being challenged.
This change brings happiness
Desire fulfilled.
Little word, *change*.
Scary.

Self-growth causes change
Sometimes good…
More empathetic of others
Sometimes bad…
Arrogance, no thought for others.
Little word, *change*
Scary.

Some *seek* change,
Not to end boredom,
But to receive rush.
They live for excitement;
Live for the next bend in the road.
Yet, others just are not equipped for change;
Change brings them fear.
Such a little word…*change*.

Lack of "change" causes cashier
To become irate.
Such a little word
Such power in a little word
You're such a tiny word
You can be positive or negative
But, I, for one don't like you very much,
Change.
January 21, 2009

Appearances and Masks

For all appearances people look normal. I look normal. I have normal hands, arms, legs and feet. And I have a normal fear of being misunderstood. I want to reach out and give people a hug but can't.

I can't express to people my feelings, so I carefully construct a façade knowing that I can't let people see behind the mask. I want my hands to hug without struggle. I want to put my arms into a coat instead of having them refuse to go in. In my bedroom after days of things building up that I wasn't even aware of, I cry out to my Heavenly Father asking sometimes, "Why?" But most of the time just asking for help. I feel like crying, but don't because I would be asked why I'm crying. So I keep my mask and appearance together and cry on the inside. I let very few people see me; people don't give me the freedom to feel what I want to feel without putting me down for it.

There are other people who walk around with masks who can pick up or put down food or drink they don't want. These masks are just as painful. I have a friend who wears masks. She is a lot like me. She only lets me and one other person see how she feels. She also has a carefully constructed cover, but I'm able to see through it. She has her physical freedom, but like me, she's looking for emotional freedom. She looks in the mirror and she believes she's too heavy. Like me, she cries on the inside looking for emotional support from her friends and all she gets is angry retorts. Our friends don't see the masks and see that we crave the freedom to do what we can, in spite of our limitations, but also crave to be loved in a tangible way. Friends try to show love with words, but words are so empty. "I love you" has been over used, and its meaning has become empty, when all we really want is a touch or a hug.

People somehow make the masks worse because their ignorance of who I am and what I can do causes self-doubts and once again, I must cover my anger.

I praise my Heavenly Father that he sees the mask for what it is and helps me know that I don't need to wear a mask.
July 25, 2009

PUMPKIN GUTS

Bright orange ripe pumpkin,
Fresh and crisp,
Just picked off the vine.
People think I'm nuts
But I'm looking forward to great fun.
Somebody takes off the top and I stick my hands in.
Joyfully I scoop out the seeds.
My hands totally consumed with orange.

"You want me to help you hold a spoon, Jenny?"
My teacher asks
I want no tool that will diminish the pleasure.
I look forward to roasting the seeds.
I enjoy removing the squishy slimy oozy pulp.

People shake their heads.
What is the fascination?
I just enjoy pumpkin guts.
August 3, 2005

REACH, REACH

Reach, reach, share my heart;
Cruelly misinterpreted.
Back down to the floor;
Must climb the mountain yet again.

My aide claims to know God's truth,
Yet, doesn't know who I am.
Sings, sleeps; always late.
Who am I? Tired of this mountain.
Pray for a change.
Now have a new aide sharing true faith.
Thank you, God, for her true worship.

I know, Lord, You give good gifts.
I hope I don't have to crash to the floor again
And climb this mountain.
But mountains and valleys are part of life,
Father,
Not of your creation

Help me not to fear the floor and love the mountain.
April 10, 2001

TOMATOES OF LIFE

Insides squished up.
Who am I?
Lifeblood dripping, oozing out,
Weakening, don't know who I am.

New place, new people, new tasks.
Cooking, cleaning, pricing groceries.
Lifeblood oozing out.
Creativity drying up.
Feelings baking away in hot sun.

Slowly feel creativity rising back within me
No longer buried by the mundane.
Creativity flowing like lifeblood.
Creativity like ripened, succulent juicy tomatoes.
Creativity in my veins
Now being expressed.

JENNY DURR

I now feel alive like fresh tomato juice
Coursing through a newly birthed plant.
No longer am I like rotten, spoiled tomatoes
Dead on their vine.
April 26, 2001

THE FORGOTTEN ONES

They like to sing, even with oxygen
Happy to see preacher friend.

Happy over hot dogs and ice cream party
Not aware politicians give parties to win votes.

They wonder
"Where's music friend?"
"He's not here today, again," says preacher friend
Curious, himself, why he's absent.

They don't understand no good-byes.
They know people go,
But they love his music and miss him.

Two friends turn to each other;
"We may be in a nursing home and
People might forget us, but God won't"
November 19, 2007

LOVE THAT WOULDN'T TAKE A BREAK

MY FRIEND GAVE ME A SHOWER IN AN UNEND- ING attempt to quiet and calm my muscles, after tor- nadoes wreaked havoc. As I lay on my bed thinking, give her a break, *let someone else deal with it,* she asked me what I was thinking. I told her I thought she should take a break, *not* from *other* people's care but just from *mine.* Her reply was: "How long would you survive without range of motion? How would you cope with those tornadoes without help?" When I explained to my friend that I did not mind sacrificing myself, she paused and with humor said, "Do me a favor, and shut the hell up!" We both burst out laugh- ing and I knew I would not need to offer my friend a break again. That night I experienced love that would- n't *take* a break.

June 10, 1997

FOOD NAMES

Corn is called…corn.
Broccoli steamed tastes good,
Simply called…broccoli.
Carrots, though, are furnishing redheads
With the name "carrot-top".
Roast beef, moist, delicious, juicy,
Turns into annoying attitude:
"What's your beef?"
Oh! Think about this,
Corn isn't just corn.
Corn has the honor of causing pain on the feet.
Constant pain causing inability to walk through life.
Scrumptious, overwhelming delicious, fantastic, brown,
Juicy pork turns into being made fun of…
"What a porker!"
Tasty bacon turns into "I can't bring home enough
bacon."
Crunchy chicken skin, meat falling off the wishbone,
Turns into "You're a chicken!"

Who turned such good food, life-giving substance,
Into such strange names and expressions?
January 5, 2008

THANKSGIVING

There is hustle and bustle.
People carving the turkey,
Asking, "Where's that knife?"
"Where is the spoon for the mashed potatoes?"
"Don't forget the cheese and potato soup,
I slaved over it all day."
People are drinking,
Having a good time.
Laughter is filling the whole dining room,
We all sit down to eat
After the hustle and bustle is finally over.
One thing is missing, though
In this huge meal of a 20-pound turkey,
Cranberry sauce, mashed potatoes, sweet potatoes,
And an assortment of pies and other desserts…
No one prays, not even me.
How could I have forgotten to give thanks…on
Thanksgiving?
December 19, 1996

CONNECTION

Voice comes over the wire;
I know in a second
This is the call I've been anticipating,
Not wanting…but anticipating.
Facilitator asks if she should give background
To non-verbal sister's dilemma.
I tell her no; I want to talk to my friend.
Oh, how I want to, I think.
I hear my friend laughing in the background
But I know it's an angry, hysterical laugh.
If she doesn't laugh, she'll cry.
I say, "Sis",
I already know
In that instant we are linked.

Like snow, facilitator melts into the background.
Painfully I ask, "Sis, did you try to get away?"
The facilitator tells me that her eyebrows are raised
Indicating a non-verbal "yes".

I'm sickened by Sis' guttural noises;
They tell me she feels shame.
But I immediately know what my next question is.
Questions don't form; they come flying off my lips.
I feel like I need to be there;
I want to protect her
But I go on...
"Do you know you're safe?"
"Do you know I love you?"
"I need to see you."
I hear pain in facilitator's voice
Relaying my messages.
I can tell facilitator wishes she didn't know
How to communicate for Sis.
Facilitator's voice is full of love for us
But repulsed by situation she's translating.
I am sickened.
Sis' guttural noises are like that of
A hurt, petrified puppy.
Not surprised to hear her leave the room,
I know she's emotionally overloaded.
I tell facilitator, "I feel sad,
Why does it have to be her?"
I want to get up there and can't.
I think to myself,
She is so sweet, so vulnerable, so full of life;
One tough cookie.
Why her?
We have such a blessed connection;
Thank you, God.

JENNY DURR

Something that is a mystery,
That goes beyond words.
I guess our connection is love.
June 19, 2002

Honoring Death

Dim gray room,
Poor lighting,
People all in a line.
I watch 5-10 minute video,
So brief.
People passing.

"Sorry for your loss"
"Sorry for your loss"
An ongoing stream.
"Sorry for your loss."

There is a collage;
People look briefly as they file by.

So much chatter in the room,
"How's your baby?"
"I haven't seen you in so long!"
"This is the second funeral in a year."

"Did you hear she's moved away?"
""It's too bad I couldn't see him before he died."
"How are you?"
"Hanging in there."

I sit watching, watching.
If you wanted to see him, why didn't you?
So busy.
People still walking through line
Never ending.
Chatter, chatter,
My loved one barely mentioned.
A social occasion.
Shouldn't this be a day of
Laughter…tears…remember when?
July 8, 2009

THE RED RIVER

Sitting at the table eating breakfast,
Leisurely munching buttered bread.
Suddenly I see a river on the table,
Not just a pretty pink,
But a deep covering red
That takes up the whole surface,
That makes it look as if the table is swimming in red.
Somebody tries to scrub away the bright red
As it continues to swim and spread across the table.
As the red partially gets wiped away,
I fear that the table will be permanently stained,
If not by a deep red, at least by a light pink red,
That looks somewhat like your tongue.
Eventually the red ceases to travel across the table
And somebody refills my glass of cranberry juice.
December 10, 1996

BRIEF BUT PRECIOUS

Friend and I kept apart, not together tonight,
I feel discouraged; won't my "tornadoes" ever end?
Suddenly I get a surprise: a treat.
My friend, my aide can feed me.
As she carefully helps me eat;
She and I bear the "tornadoes" together.
We don't have long, but we enjoy the meal.
Brief but precious.

Later I'm terrified, petrified, by my "tornadoes".
My friend arrives again, unexpectedly
And we conquer the "tornadoes" together.
Not having long, she gently talks with me;
Reasons, calms, reassures,
Even though I am too frightened to hear
And accept her words as truth.
Again, I am thankful for the time we shared.
Brief but precious.
February 13, 1997

MATH

Math has a special vocabulary.
Numerator.
Denominator.
Equation.
Expression.
Variable.
Math does help you find out
How much you need to pay to eat.
It does help pharmacists
Figure out medicine formulas.
But other than that, what's Algebra for?
It fills a ridiculous place.

English also has its own unique vocabulary.
Articles.
Conjunctions.
Predicates.
Adjectives.
Naming this vocabulary can be boring.

But each word you connect
Whether it's a noun or adjective sends a message.
The message can make someone
Cry, laugh, throw something.
But math doesn't touch the soul.
October 26, 2006

What Do Jesus' Hands Look Like?

Jesus' hands gladly wipe away a tear.
Jesus' hands are gentle
When they are helping someone
Who cannot take care of themselves.
A person can sense that his hands really care.

Jesus' hands stop their busy schedule
To give someone a hug.
Jesus' hands give someone a pat on the shoulder
Or reassuring comforting touch.

Thank you, God, for all Your Hands.
September 5, 1993

The Beauty of Silence

I need to tell you something, but I'm unable to; I'm too full of pain. We sit in my dining room together, seeing each other after so long. I need to tell you something but I still hold back. After you ask me what's wrong many times with just your eyes, you begin to get angry. I see the worry on your face and in your eyes, but still refuse to open up, afraid of what you'll say. You slowly type, laboriously, on your device. You say "I'm sick of you".

I'm stunned; you almost never use your device, and when you do you never use full sentences. I know your news must be bad, but I still don't open myself to you. After typing the words, "our friend sick", and trying to get me to tell you what's happening yet again, you back away from me. "I don't know what to do with my life". I tell you I'm sorry for not opening up. I can't move to you; we both just sit there. Then I say to you again "I'm sorry, I just can't take it; I can't take my life right now." You drive up to me, I read your face; it's saying "it's okay".

You may not even remember that day, but, after that day I began thinking about how we don't have to use words. I am so thankful that we just know; we don't have to use a whole bunch of words that don't come out right.

December 27, 2001

Revised June 24, 2009

Big "D"

Bright sun,
Birds singing,
Bright red birds flying around.
Traveling,
Traveling,
Clear road.
This is such a nice Sunday.

She touches her 'other half',
Wanting to hold on to these good feelings.
Without warning, she hits a pothole!
She shakes her head,
Hoping there won't be another one.
She hopes she can hold on to this good day.
She needs a good day.

Clear road.
Slow, even, flat surface.
Other traffic moving along at healthy pace.

Suddenly she hears a thud;
Tire hits a rut and car swerves.
Seeing a sign, she shakes her head.

Eerily, the birds stop their singing...

She fearfully grips the wheel.
Seeing her worried face
'Other half' pats her shoulder.
"Can't happen, you won't miss another road sign,
hon."
He hopes he's right.

She looks straight ahead,
Determined not to miss another sign.
Suddenly tire hits a nail.
Hearing a slow leak; she drives anyway.

She wonders
Where did the birds go?
Not realizing they flew away.

She makes a wrong turn,
Wishing her loved one could drive.
She wants to keep it a good day
But she knows she's losing the way.

She watches her shaking hands..

Suddenly the streets are dark gray, narrow.
There is no room to move the car
No room to move.
A sign blazing
Bad neighborhood
Bad neighborhood
She struggles to turn around.

Traveling down a smooth stretch,
Steering stably,
She drives securely,
Thankful she left *bad neighborhood*.

Without warning she makes a wrong turn
Re-entering *bad neighborhood*.
This time she can't leave…can't leave.

Quickly, partner points frantically.
Looking, she sees a fence with a big red sign
Depression Neighborhood Ahead.
Desperately trying to control the car,
She hits the fence!
February 26, 2009
Revised July 15, 2009

CHRISTMAS BAKING

Delicious smells fills the whole house.
Wonderful fattening treats call my name.
Fattening, fattening;
Each treats a pound, which I ignore.
Turn on Christmas Carols.
I sing with my aide as she works
Beating, mixing, sniffing, sneaking, tasting,
German chocolate cake, peanut butter cookies.
Oh how delicious!
She cleans up the dishes and we say Merry
Christmas!
December 16, 2004

DIFFERENT HAIR, SAME OLD ME

"You look cute,
You look more mature,
You look like a grown-up woman", people say.
Who is this in the mirror, I think,
Maybe I'll start wearing rouge.

"You need to get it cut shorter."
"I just had it cut,
I don't want to get it cut again."
"Can't you take any constructive criticism?
It needs to be styled more,
There's too much on your neck."
It's my hair and I don't want to get it cut anymore."
"Can't you take criticism?"
Different hair, same old me.
August 20, 2002

Why Can't He Have Just One Meal?

I sit at the dinner table with my friend; his innocent face eager to eat. One of the Aides goes down a mental list of favorite, desired concoctions, finally hits on the one that strikes his fancy tonight. He wants to eat; he is eager to eat; his eyes go up at the suggestion of doing so. He seeks a cupcake which looks good. But, sadly, after the Aide brings the meal he longs for and prepares the cupcake with milk so he could swallow it; my friend is only able to take a few bites.

For whatever reason, his stomach or painful throat muscles refuse to allow him the pleasure I take for granted. The complaining I do because the food isn't the way I like it makes me feel guilty. I think about how he eats in pain almost always and wonder why he can't have just one meal.
September 26, 1996

A LITTLE GRACE

(Dedicated to an Aide who took care of me and
helped me cope during a very hard time in my life)

Every time you hold me and tell me it will be okay,
I see God's Grace.

Every time you say tears are good and let me cry,
I see God's Grace.

Every time you say, "I'm with you, we'll get through
this together",
I see God's Grace.

Every time you watch me suffer through my tornadoes,
I see God's Grace.

Every time you tell me, "I think I know what's both-
ering you",
I see God's Grace.

Every time we laugh together,
I see God's Grace.
March 4, 1996
*Originally published in a church bulletin.
Revised October 28, 2009

BLESSINGS

I stare at a yellow rose,
Its' petals so crisp,
So uniquely formed,
That's a blessing.
I look up at the blue sky,
The Colorado Mountains,
The immensity of Pike's Peak.
That's a blessing.
I stare at an orange and brown Monarch with awe,
That's a blessing.
My friend crosses my mind,
That's a blessing.

My friend does my hair in just the right way,
So it doesn't smother me all night long,
That's a blessing.
My friend's hands are gentle,
While relaxing me and relieving my pain,
That's a blessing.

My friend helps me respect myself,
That's a blessing.
My friend always checks on me to see if I'm asleep,
That's a blessing.
My friend always tries to give me wisdom,
And make me laugh,
That's a blessing.

A secretary friend
Helps me E-mail,
That's a blessing.
My friend with her new baby,
Always talks to me about life,
That's a blessing.
My Mom drives me from place to place,
That's a blessing.
My doctor always tries to teach me skills
To respect myself and listens,
Even if no one else does,
That's a blessing.
God is a blessing.
He is my ultimate blessing.
He gives me all my blessings.
April 8, 1997

Defined

There are many ways to define people.
White, black, yellow, short, fat.
Some fearful, some sad.
Some hopeless pessimists.
Still others judgmental and annoying.
Some full of hate.
Some insecure foolish put downers.
Selfish, tactless, stubborn.
And others just weird.

Still some are funny and cheerful.
Vulnerable, talented.
Yet still others busy, loving, and giving.
Some wonderful encouragers.
Some gruff bears who give great hugs.
Others are fighters, strength seekers.
Some are helpful and challenging.
Others are loving protectors.

Whether we use one word or ten to define ourselves,
We are the Lord God's creation
And defined by one word…human!
May 18, 2009
Revised June 10, 2009

Manufactured By: RR Donnelley
                     Breinigsville, PA USA
                     December, 2010